21 TO ONENESS

Beating the Odds For a Healthy Marriage Devotional

Geoff Gibbs Jr.
&
Jasmine M. Gibbs

TABLE OF CONTENTS

Dedication	3
Introduction	4
Day 1: Fighting The Right Fight	6
Day 2: The Myth of Perfection	10
Day 3: The Power of the Triangle	14
Day 4: The Art of Effective Communication: A Lesson in Listening	17
Day 5: Marriage Equals Oneness (but not Necessarily Sameness)	20
Day 6: Are We There Yet?: Broken Trust	22
Day 7: Rebuilding Trust: Heal, Restore, and Grow	26
Day 8: Communication That Connects	29
Day 9: Your Marriage Needs Community	32
Day 10: A Lifetime of Commitment: Insights from a 63-Year Marriage	35
Day 11: Building on a Firm Foundation	39
Day 12: The Art of Fighting Fair	41
Day 13: Love Has A Language	44
Day 14: Navigating the Challenges of Marriage (The Husband's Perspective)	47
Day 15: Navigating Identity and Expectations in Marriage (The Wife's Perspective)	50
Day 16: Nurturing Intimacy in Marriage	54
Day 17: Marriage and Ministry: A Journey of Love and Service	57
Day 18: Blended Families: Fostering Growth and Resilience	60
Day 19: Your Marriage Is Worth The Investment	63
Day 20: Being a Husband	65
Day 21: The Power of Help	68

DEDICATION

To our children: Geoffrey and Jackson you have become the impetus for our continued desire to cultivate a love that is enduring and fruitful. Thank you for being the most amazing sons. You are truly the best gifts to us. You are our heart and soul.

To our parents and grandparents, thank you for your enduring love, sacrifice and lasting support. We could not be who we are without you.

To the couples who have poured into our union, thank you for seeing in us what we could not always see in ourselves, and for sharing your love, pain, triumphs, and hope with us.

To the ones who have been responsible with sharing our sacred space and provided us with safety, wisdom, guidance along the way, we offer our deepest gratitude and appreciation to you.

To the couples searching for God in their marriage, take heart, He can be found. God honors marriage and is committed to the success of it. Invite Him in.

INTRODUCTION

Let's face it, according to mainstream culture and statistics, the odds are stacked against marriage. When the odds are not in your favor, it can feel daunting to approach the idea of having a life-giving, long-lasting, and fulfilling marriage. We have certainly faced our fair share of challenges that threatened the longevity and success of our marriage. Embarking upon this journey together to open up and share some of the lessons we have learned has taken some courage and an abandonment of the need for privacy.

Privacy has been a tremendous asset to our marriage. As we have navigated the ups and downs of two individuals becoming one, we have found that working together outside the view of others gives us the freedom to make mistakes and, more importantly, to learn from them. The broader public didn't need to know the specifics of our insecurities, the areas of deep brokenness that we brought into our marriage as individuals, or the seasons where we were just fighting to get from one day to the next. We kept these tender areas close to each other and a select few third parties as we grew to ensure we didn't taint what we shared. We were very protective of this beautiful gift we had been given.

Although we valued our privacy, we quickly learned that there were key struggles we faced that actually turned out to be common in marriages. We realized that we could have benefited from the testimonies and strategies of other couples who had been through similar situations and, as a result, grew from them. We often wondered if certain mistakes could have been preempted positively had we had the benefit of others who put biblical keys into practice and experienced success in those areas. We began to feel a burden for other couples who may be fighting the same battles alone, and so we have taken brave steps to share some of the treasures of our hearts.

In 2018, we approached our 15th wedding anniversary, and we spent time reflecting on our journey together in getting to that milestone. One Sunday afternoon while sitting on our couch, we picked up our phone and pressed record. This began a 15-day journey leading up to our anniversary date where we committed to sharing some of the insights and experiences (on Facebook) that have been helpful to us along the way. Although we didn't consider ourselves marriage "experts," we thought it could be helpful to those we knew. Now, 21 years into our marriage, we decided to embark on another journey to share more about those insights and experiences that have colored our now 26-year relationship. This 21-day marriage devotional is the fruit of that effort.

Over the next 21 days, it is our prayer that you take time to have discussions, write notes, and prayerfully learn how the tools we share can help enhance and grow more fruit in your marriage. We are confident the topics and issues addressed are common to most marriages and can be beneficial if you have been married for six months or 60 years. In this devotional, you will hear perspectives from both of us—the man (Geoff) and woman (Jasmine) to find areas of commonality and relevance that can help to give language to your individual concerns. We want you to have the opportunity to get a complete picture of both sides of the marriage story. After each day of sharing wisdom and insight, you have been provided a section to answer questions and reflect on that day's devotion. As you actively engage with this devotional, it is our prayer that you will reap the full benefit of our 21 years of marital trials and triumphs. Beyond what we may know or understand, we believe your willingness to honor God in your marriage through engaging with this devotional tool will allow God's power to grow, heal, and restore the areas you offer to Him. God honors marriages that seek to honor Him, so get ready for His life-changing power to help you in ways that only He can.

Geoff & Jasmine

DAY 1: FIGHTING THE RIGHT FIGHT

Heavenly Father, we come before You with open hearts, ready to embark on this journey of love, marriage, and life. Help us embrace the vulnerability that strengthens our relationships and draws us closer to You and each other. Amen.

1 Corinthians 13:4-7 (NIV) - "Love is patient, love is kind. It does not envy, it does not boast, it is not proud. It does not dishonor others, it is not self-seeking, it is not easily angered, it keeps no record of wrongs. Love does not delight in evil but rejoices with the truth. It always protects, always trusts, always hopes, always perseveres."

Ephesians 6:12-13 (NLT) "For we are not fighting against flesh and blood enemies, but against evil rulers and authorities of the unseen world, against mighty powers in this dark world, against evil spirits in the heavenly places. Stand your ground putting on the belt of truth and the body armor of God's righteousness."

Geoff

"You're never here for me when I need you."

"You think money is the answer for everything."

"You don't listen to me."

"You always take their side of the story."

"You aren't an adequate provider."

"You aren't good enough."

Defensiveness is a stumbling block in the journey toward healthy marriage. This is an issue because we tend to fight back when we feel vulnerable or unsafe, even against the ones we love. Early in my marriage, I wish I had known that I didn't have to defend myself against the person I loved, especially when I felt attacked. I wish I had known to return grace to my spouse when I felt attacked, and that pausing to listen to what was being said behind her words was the best way to respond. There are two reasons for this.

First, I found that there were times when my insecurities yielded a defensiveness that was the filter through which I processed feedback from my wife. My defensive filter caused me to hear the contents of her heart as assaults on my intentions. I heard things that weren't said, and I completely missed genuine expressions of her heart in a given situation. As a result, I processed her expressions for something she needed more of as statements about what I was not providing or could not provide. My insecurities caused me to hear accusations about what I was not, rather than what she needed.

The second reason for returning grace when faced with an offense is based upon this truth - our spouses are human. They can and will make mistakes. They will cause us harm, even when they love us. They will disappoint us. They will lash out. They may even say things in anger that betray their true feelings for us. This inevitably means there will be times when they will go on the offensive and attack us. It means that conflicts will arise when they are the source of our offense. These are the times when I struggled to offer grace-filled responses the most. My sense of justice overruled my God honoring requirement to offer grace.

Instead, returning grace, even when attacked, proved better in the long run.

"A gentle answer deflects anger, but harsh words make tempers flare."
Proverbs 15:1 NLT

The reality of our human frailty is this type of grace isn't always easy to offer in the heat of the moment, but it yields results.

This commitment to returning grace is more feasible when there is confidence that the person you are with is the one God sent to you.

This is more difficult when you marry someone you picked, but aren't confident God picked because, well, you could be wrong!

If, however, you can rest assured that this person you are with is ultimately FOR you, then you can be vulnerable and not feel as if you have to always defend yourself against them.

I recall a time when I would meet conflict with retaliation, especially toward the woman I loved. Yet, over time, wisdom found its way into my heart, teaching me the immeasurable value of grace. During this time of reflection, I want to remind you that in the heat of disagreements, responding with love, grace, and humility often yields the most beautiful resolutions.

Jasmine

Early in our marriage, it would have helped to know that fighting TOGETHER is more beneficial to the health and well-being of our marriage than fighting against each other. I wish I knew that I didn't have to treat my husband as an enemy combatant in the face of conflict. The true fight has ALWAYS been and will always be against the enemy of our soul and our union. I oftentimes would respond out of my need to protect myself against my husband. I dealt strongly with the fear that he would hurt me and I struggled to feel safe. This caused me to operate out of a "fight or flight" mentality. Fear would motivate my responses towards him in times of conflict. You cannot successfully win in your marriage if you are not willing to be vulnerable with your partner. This, however, requires safety and trust in each other. You must see your union as the thing you are both emotionally and mentally invested in. You have to see your union as worth fighting FOR.

I want to emphasize the importance of standing together as a united front against life's challenges. We have fought for our partnership in the face of great adversity. This speaks volumes about the strength of our commitment to one another. Our love, fortified by unity, stands as a testament that marriage is not just the joining of two individuals, but the union of two souls navigating life's intricate path, hand in hand.

REALITY CHECK - Your partner is NOT your adversary, but the union does have an actual adversary.

You should keep him in view when considering the nexus of the assaults coming against your marriage.

A three-fold cord is not easily broken.

"Two people are better off than one, for they can help each other succeed. If one person falls, the other can reach out and help. But someone who falls alone is in real trouble. Likewise, two people lying close together can keep each other warm. But how can one be warm alone? A person standing alone can be attacked and defeated, but two can stand back-to-back and conquer. Three are even better, for a triple-braided cord is not easily broken." Ecclesiastes 4:9-12 NLT

Keeping a perspective of the proper third party (God) and expelling the illegal third party (the adversary) is critical

Prioritize the bond that your two souls share. With a shared heart, we encourage you to nurture your relationship with diligence, for it is through these efforts that the flame of love continues to glow. The warmth and light it radiates inspires us to kindle the flames of our own relationships.

Reflect on 1 Corinthians 13:4-7: "Love is patient, love is kind... It always protects, always trusts, always hopes, always perseveres." How does this scripture guide us in embracing vulnerability and strengthening our relationships?

Dear Lord, we pray for the courage to embrace vulnerability in our relationships. Teach us to respond with love and humility. Help us stand united in the face of challenges. May Your love guide us on this journey of love, marriage, and life. May the lessons from today draw us closer to You and to one another. In Jesus' name, we pray. Amen.

REFLECTIVE APPLICATION

Take time to reflect on a recent conflict or challenge in your relationship. Consider how responding with love, grace, and humility might have a positive impact. Share your thoughts and insights with your loved one, and discuss ways to strengthen your bond.

1. Have you ever faced conflicts in your relationship where responding with love, grace, and humility made a significant difference? Share your experience.

2. How do you prioritize the bond in your marriage, ensuring that love continues to grow and flourish?

_____
_____
_____
_____
_____
_____
_____
_____
_____
_____
_____
_____
_____
_____
_____
_____
_____
_____
_____
_____
_____
_____
_____
_____
_____
_____
_____

DAY 2: THE MYTH OF PERFECTION

Heavenly Father, we come before You as imperfect and heavily flawed individuals seeking wisdom and understanding in our marriage. Help us to not live in bondage to the myth of a perfect marriage. We recognize our need for You, the One who is perfect. Help us to daily embrace our need for Your grace and give us the desire to follow Your example of perfect love. In Jesus' name, we pray, Amen.

Ecclesiastes 7:20 (NIV) - "Indeed, there is no one on earth who is righteous, no one who does what is right and never sins."

Everyone loves mermaids, leprechauns, and unicorns, but no one has actually seen them. The same can be said about "perfect" marriages. Everyone loves weddings, and everyone adores love stories; people get excited about #marriagegoals and the presentation of a perfectly crafted highlight reel of marital bliss, but the reality is there is no perfect marriage. It does not exist. It is a myth.

When we get married, we do so from a place of love and inspiration, but once two imperfect people decide to come together in matrimony, 'poof' - the myth of a perfect marriage disappears. What is left are two imperfect individuals who are trying to build and live life together.

Jasmine

The cultural expectations of perfection place an undue burden on many marriages. In the age of social media, we have been inundated with the highlight reel of most relationships we see play out before us. Unfortunately, this has contributed to many having a skewed expectation of reality, especially in marriage. Most people are not "posting" their recent argument, their financial struggles, their struggles with intimacy, their struggles with in-law drama, or their private conversations about divorce. The truth is, some days are harder than others in marriage and some days you just may entertain the thought of quitting. The reality is no one lives in a perpetual highlight reel. The nature of life is that it is filled with complex moments. No one's life is full of high moments and completely absent of low moments. Do not get me wrong, there is nothing wrong with desiring to live a life that contains sincere happiness, joy, and fulfillment, but longing for perfection will inevitably leave us disappointed. Perfection does not exist. The same truth applies to marriage - we should desire real joy in marriage, and we should look forward to a life of love and fulfillment with our spouses. We should focus on building a marriage that works perfectly for us and our spouses.

This is an issue for many couples who think there is something wrong with their marriage because it isn't a perfect portrayal of the love stories they have seen played out on TV or social media. When our spouses don't exhibit the same qualities we have seen in our favorite actors, we feel they are the problem. Their imperfections become the basis for our erroneous assessment of the lack of health in our marriage.

Geoff

Marriage is a beautiful union that brings two imperfect individuals together in love and companionship. However, in our society, there is often an unrealistic expectation of a perfect marriage, fueled by fairy tales and media portrayals. Today we focus on the myth of the perfect marriage and shed light on the importance of focusing on a healthy and fulfilling relationship with your spouse instead.

It is essential to acknowledge that there is no such thing as a perfect marriage. Just like mythical creatures such as mermaids, leprechauns, and unicorns, the idea of a perfect marriage remains elusive. While everyone desires a harmonious and blissful partnership, the reality is that, once two imperfect individuals come together, the notion of perfection dissipates. Instead, you are left with flawed human beings navigating life together, striving to cultivate a life of love and commitment.

In our culture, we are constantly bombarded with portrayals of the "highlight reel" of life through social media, movies, and books. This inundation can contribute to skewed expectations and a distorted perception of reality. It is crucial to understand that nobody lives a perfect life, just as nobody lives in a perfect marriage. While you can find happiness, contentment, and joy in your marriage, perfection does not exist. Unrealistic expectations can lead to disappointment and a sense of inadequacy, both individually and within the relationship.

We often teach young girls about the fairy tale idea of a perfect marriage, where they find their Prince Charming and live happily ever after. However, this narrative fails to acknowledge the challenges and complexities of real-life relationships. When individuals wake up to the reality of a partnership with imperfect human beings, disillusionment can set in. This can lead to a culture of cutting and running, believing that if the marriage isn't perfect, it is not worth pursuing.

Amidst the myth of the perfect marriage, we want to encourage couples to focus on building a healthy relationship instead. Understand that imperfections and challenges are a part of every relationship. Rather than comparing your marriage to others or seeking an unattainable ideal, invest in the health of your partnership. Just like nurturing a plant, a marriage requires time, effort, and care to flourish. By focusing on the well-being of both individuals involved, you can create a relationship that is perfect for you.

It is crucial to dispel the myth of the perfect marriage and embrace the reality of an imperfect yet fulfilling partnership. Let go of the unrealistic expectations perpetuated by fairy tales and media. Instead, focus on building a healthy relationship that nurtures both individuals involved. Remember, there is no such thing as a perfect marriage, but there is a marriage that can be perfect for you. Embrace the imperfections, invest in the well-being of your partnership, and strive for a love that grows and evolves.

"Three different times I begged the Lord to take it away. Each time he said, 'My grace is all you need. My power works best in weakness.' So now I am glad to boast about my weaknesses so that the power of Christ can work through me. That's why I take pleasure in my weaknesses, and in the insults, hardships, persecutions, and troubles that I suffer for Christ. For when I am weak, then I am strong."

2 Corinthians 12:8-10 NLT

Reflect on Ecclesiastes 7:20: "Indeed, there is no one on earth who is righteous, no one who does what is right and never sins." How does this verse remind us of our imperfections and the importance of grace in our relationship?

We want to encourage couples to know they are not alone in their imperfect marriage. We want to implore you to shift your focus from a "perfect" marriage to a healthy marriage. Healthy marriages are built by healthy individuals who invest in their marriage.

You've heard the saying "The grass isn't always greener on the other side, rather the grass is greener when we water it." Nurturing our relationship helps us to have a healthy marriage. Nurturing our marriage helps us build a marriage that "fits" us: one that is "perfect" for us.

Heavenly Father, we thank You for Your grace and understanding in our imperfect lives and marriages. Help us let go of the myth of perfection and embrace the beauty of what is authentic and imperfect. Help us to make allowance for one another's imperfections through grace and love. Guide us in building a healthy and fulfilling marriage that is a reflection of Your love and grace. Help us cultivate a healthy and loving marriage that reflects Your love for us. In Jesus' name, we pray. Amen.

REFLECTIVE APPLICATION

Take time to have an open and honest conversation with your spouse about unrealistic expectations of perfection in your marriage. Share how you can work together to embrace imperfection and build a healthy relationship.

1. Have you ever felt the pressure to have a "perfect" marriage? How did this affect your relationship?

2. How can you and your spouse embrace the imperfections in your marriage and focus on building a healthy relationship?

_____
_____
_____
_____
_____
_____
_____
_____
_____
_____
_____
_____
_____
_____
_____
_____
_____
_____
_____
_____
_____
_____
_____
_____

DAY 3: THE POWER OF THE TRIANGLE

Dear Heavenly Father, we come before you today with hearts full of gratitude for the gift of marriage. We thank You for the opportunity to gather and reflect on the sacred union You have designed. May this time together deepen our understanding of how to honor You and one another in our marriage. In Jesus' name, we pray. Amen.

Proverbs 3:5-6 (NIV)
  "Trust in the Lord with all your heart and lean not on your own understanding; in all your ways submit to him, and he will make your paths straight."

Jasmine

It was a weekday night, and we were taking a break from our college studies. We sat at a table for 2 in Fellini's Pizza near midtown Atlanta. Geoff reached for a napkin and pulled out a pen. He proceeded to draw a triangle. At this point, although smitten by him, I was still getting to know him. So I didn't know how to take his decision to practice drawing his shapes at the table in the middle of what I thought was good conversation. He proceeded to write "God" at the top of the triangle and then "you and "me" at the 2 angles below. He began to share his heart about what he believed would guarantee longevity in our relationship. Although we were only boyfriend and girlfriend, at the time his admonishment was: If we focus not just on each other, but rather on God first as we grow to know one another, we would benefit from having something that would stand the test of time. I had never heard this concept from anyone, let alone a guy I dated. This not only intrigued me, but it hooked me. I was completely sold, and the rest was history.

Geoff

The Felini's Pizza date happened over 25 years ago and the concept of the triangle remains relevant and noteworthy. We tend to set our focus on the one we love, are pursuing, and want to spend all of our time with. To exclusively focus on each other tends to give way to infatuation and a level of blindness. There is nothing wrong with focusing on each other, but this should not be absent from God as the third party in our relationship. In learning how to please God together, He teaches us how to please one another. Let me say this- you will fail many times at trying to please the one you are with from your own strength and understanding. Keeping a closeness to God and allowing the character of Christ to be developed in you individually will draw you closer to one another in the relationship.

Let's take a deeper dive. Marriage is a sacred union that requires constant effort and commitment to thrive. In our journey as a couple, we have discovered a powerful concept that has shaped the foundation of our relationship: the triangle. This metaphor represents the dynamic interplay between God, husband, and wife. By placing God at the pinnacle and focusing on growing closer to Him together, we have witnessed the transformative impact it has had on our marriage.

The triangle symbolizes the pursuit of wholeness and progressive improvement in a marriage. As believers, we understand that aligning our lives with God's purpose is essential to becoming our best selves. By continuously striving to become more God-like and Christ-like, we create a solid foundation on which our relationship can flourish. The triangle reminds us that marriage is not solely about the connection between spouses; rather, it is about vertical growth towards God, which in turn deepens our bond with each other.

An exclusive focus on each other may lead to stagnation and complacency in a marriage. When all our attention is directed towards our spouse, we may inadvertently stop progressing as individuals. By recognizing the danger of this horizontal focus, we can shift our perspective towards personal growth and improvement. As we become the best versions of ourselves, we bring more to the table, offering our spouses the love, grace, and security they deserve.

While striving for growth and improvement is essential, we must remember that it is only through God's grace and guidance that we can truly succeed. We acknowledge that we are imperfect beings, incapable of meeting all our spouse's needs. The grace of God sustains us and enables us to honor and cherish our partners in a way that surpasses our natural limitations.

Marriage serves as a refining process, exposing our flaws and imperfections. It acts as a mirror, revealing areas in our lives that require honesty, submission, and growth. By embracing this refining process rather than resisting it, we can create an environment that fosters personal and relational growth.

Reflect on Proverbs 3:5-6 "Trust in the Lord with all your heart and lean not on your own understanding; in all your ways submit to him, and he will make your paths straight."

Heavenly Father, we thank You for the insights and wisdom shared today as we explored the power of the triangle in marriage. We pray that these reflections will take root in our hearts and bear fruit in our relationships. May Your love and grace be the cornerstone of every union. In the name of Jesus, we pray. Amen.

REFLECTIVE APPLICATION

Think about your marriage as a refining process. What imperfections or challenges have you encountered that ultimately led to growth and improvement in your relationship? How can you embrace this refining process going forward?

1. How can you and your spouse actively pursue vertical growth, aligning your lives more closely with God's purpose, and how might this strengthen your marriage?

2. Reflect on your marriage. Consider how strengthening your personal individual relationship with God can strengthen the bond in your marriage. Are there areas where you've been exclusively focusing on each other to the detriment of your individual growth and development? How can you strike a better balance between your focus on each other and growing together in God?

DAY 4: THE ART OF EFFECTIVE COMMUNICATION: A LESSON IN LISTENING

Gracious Father, we come before You seeking guidance and wisdom in how to have communication that is effective and beneficial to our growth as a unit. Help us to truly hear and understand one another, fostering deeper connections and healthier relationships. Let our communication efforts be guided by the desire for mutual resolution and not just the need to be "right" or "get our way." In Jesus' name we pray, Amen.

James 1:19 (NIV) - "My dear brothers and sisters, take note of this: Everyone should be quick to listen, slow to speak, and slow to become angry."

Effective communication is often hailed as the cornerstone of healthy relationships. Yet, how often do we misinterpret or misunderstand the words of our loved ones? Sometimes men "tap out" of the communication process when there are "too many" words expressed by their spouse. Communication challenges can make spouses feel as if the other is speaking a foreign language. It can make understanding seem impossible. One of the most critical components of effective communication is hearing, that is, being able to adequately hear what the other is saying. Communication attempts can fall into disarray when we make assumptions and decisions based on what we "think" the other person is saying. Effective communication requires patience and understanding, especially when faced with language barriers, significant disagreements, or distractions.

It's important to learn how to effectively communicate with your partner and be willing to adjust how you communicate for the other person to understand what you are trying to say. It can be frustrating when attempting to communicate with your spouse and they over-talk you or only stay quiet until it is time to offer their rebuttal. Many have a common tendency to listen with the intent to respond, rather than listening to gain understanding, which often leads to more misunderstandings and arguments. Some communicators have a fast delivery, and, if your spouse takes longer to process a thought, there could be a temptation to grow impatient with them. This can often lead to one spouse making assumptions about what the other spouse is trying to communicate and rushing to a response. In reality, a missing link causes a breach in communication. Sometimes, we can be so distracted by differing communication styles that we never address the true point of the conversation.

Effective communication goes beyond verbal exchanges, however, as it emphasizes the significance of nonverbal cues and body language. There is an inherent challenge for many couples to interpret these physical and tonal cues accurately.

The importance of effective communication within the context of marriage is especially highlighted in conflict. Emotionally charged language can be used as a weapon rather than a mechanism to foster shared understanding, so both partners need to communicate to comprehend the message coming from their spouse, rather than seeking to win arguments. This is not, by any means, simple or easy, so we want to stress the necessity of these two focus areas - recalling the shared mission of your marriage, and being fully persuaded of the importance of submitting to God, which brings order and clarity to the communication process.

Pursue effective communication. Be slow to speak, quick to listen, and truly hear the heart of your partner. By understanding the importance of active listening and seeking guidance from God, couples can overcome barriers and foster healthier and more meaningful connections.

Reflect on James 1:19: "My dear brothers and sisters, take note of this: Everyone should be quick to listen, slow to speak, and slow to become angry." How can you apply this verse to your communication with your spouse?

Heavenly Father, grant us the wisdom and patience to be active listeners in our relationships. Help us to truly hear and understand one another, fostering deeper connections and resolving conflicts with grace. May our communication be guided by Your Word and the love we share. We thank You for the gift of communication and the opportunity to connect with our spouse. Help us to be patient listeners who seek understanding and unity in our relationships. In Jesus' name, we pray. Amen.

REFLECTIVE APPLICATION

Choose a moment each day to practice active listening with your spouse. Focus on truly hearing and understanding their thoughts and feelings, and seek opportunities to improve your communication through listening.

1. Have you ever experienced a miscommunication with your spouse due to assumptions or distractions? How did it impact your relationship?

2. How can you practice active listening in your daily interactions, especially in moments of disagreement or misunderstanding?

DAY 5: MARRIAGE EQUALS ONENESS (BUT NOT NECESSARILY SAMENESS)

Merciful Father, we seek Your guidance as we explore the importance of choosing wisely in marriage. Help us make deliberate and thoughtful decisions in our pursuit of a fulfilling partnership. Amen.

Proverbs 18:22 (NIV) - "He who finds a wife finds what is good and receives favor from the LORD."

Matthew 19: 5+6 "5 And he said, "'This explains why a man leaves his father and mother and is joined to his wife, and the two are united into one. 6 Since they are no longer two but one, let no one split apart what God has joined together."

Maintaining individual identities while embracing oneness is a key aspect of identity within marriage. It is essential for couples to acknowledge and honor each other's need for personal growth, hobbies, and interests, nurturing their individual identities. Simultaneously, open communication and mutual understanding are crucial in navigating the balance between self-care and oneness. Through ongoing dialogue and a shared vision, couples can explore creative solutions that foster personal growth while maintaining a strong foundation of unity within the marriage. (We will talk more about the loss of identity in our day 15 devotion from a wife's perspective.)

Love is undeniably the foundation of any successful marriage, but it alone cannot sustain a relationship. Both partners must be willing to invest time, effort, and energy into nurturing their union. Love should be complemented by mutual respect, shared values, and a commitment to personal and joint growth. By prioritizing these factors over external pressures or societal expectations, you can build a strong foundation for a lasting and fulfilling marriage.

The invitation to oneness in marriage is in actuality an invitation to die... Dying to self. This may seem unappealing and could cause a potential aversion to marriage for some. However, the process of dying to self is in actuality an invitation to gain more through giving; and an invitation to willingly release our selfishness to receive the gift of oneness. Consider financial investments - when we invest, we release funds and diminish liquidity in the short term, to receive a return on that in the long term. While we don't consider investing a liability, we should also view the relinquishing of certain freedoms in marriage as an investment in oneness that will yield a beneficial return.

Our Father, guide us in making wise and deliberate choices in our pursuit of a fulfilling marriage. Help us to prioritize self-care, open communication, and a shared vision within our relationships. May our marriages be built on a strong foundation of love, mutual respect, and joint growth. Help us make thoughtful decisions that lead to fulfilling and harmonious relationships. In Jesus' name, we pray. Amen.

REFLECTIVE APPLICATION

Reflect on Proverbs 18:22: "He who finds a wife finds what is good and receives favor from the LORD." How does this verse emphasize the importance of making a wise choice in a life partner?

1A. Take some time to reflect on your own or with your partner about the qualities and values most important to you in a life partner. Consider how these factors contribute to a fulfilling and balanced marriage.

1B. Take a moment to share with your partner about the qualities they possess that have added great value to your life and the union.

Reflect on Matthew 19: 5+6 "5 And he said, "'This explains why a man leaves his father and mother and is joined to his wife, and the two are united into one. 6 Since they are no longer two but one, let no one split apart what God has joined together."

2. How can open communication and a shared vision help you maintain a balance between individuality and oneness within your marriage?

DAY 6: ARE WE THERE YET?: BROKEN TRUST

Merciful Father, we come before You seeking guidance and strength as we explore the challenging path of rebuilding trust that has been broken in the relationship. Grant us the wisdom to navigate this journey with sincerity, love and forgiveness. Amen.

Psalms 147:3 (NLT) "He heals the brokenhearted and bandages their wounds."

Proverbs 3:5-6 (NIV) - "Trust in the LORD with all your heart and lean not on your own understanding; in all your ways submit to him, and he will make your paths straight.

Every marriage has had to wrestle with the issue of trust at some point.

How this topic is addressed can determine success or failure in the relationship.

Every parent who has ever had to do a long road trip with their child can attest to hearing this universal question: Are we there yet? Hearing this question on a road trip is annoying after you hear it one too many times. Can you imagine the impact of hearing this question after a violation of trust in marriage?

When trust is violated, the one who initiated the breach can often wonder when this part is going to be done. Will we ever get past this? When are you going to trust me again? Are we there yet?

Trust is a fundamental pillar of successful relationships, and, when it is broken, the path to rebuilding it can be arduous. On day six, we journey through essential steps and principles necessary to restore trust and foster stronger bonds between couples.

The journey towards rebuilding trust begins with genuine repentance. Those who have caused harm must take full responsibility for their actions, expressing sincere remorse for the pain inflicted. This crucial step involves acknowledging the violation and making a firm commitment to change. Without repentance, rebuilding trust becomes nearly impossible. It sets the foundation for healing and paves the way for personal growth and transformation.

Transparency is a critical element in rebuilding trust. Both parties must embrace complete honesty, leaving no room for doubt or deception. The offender that breached trust must openly address the areas where trust was violated, as well as maintain transparency in all other aspects of their lives. This level of openness helps the offended party regain confidence and creates a sense of security within the relationship. Transparency lays bare the truth and dispels any lingering whispers of deception.

When rebuilding trust, it is vital to discard preconceived timelines. Healing cannot be rushed, and forgiveness cannot be demanded or expected immediately. Patience is key. The process of rebuilding trust takes time and effort. By relinquishing the need for immediate resolution and focusing on doing the necessary work, both individuals can begin to restore trust and experience personal growth and transformation.

Trust is not solely tested through infidelity; it permeates various areas of a relationship. Financial concerns, external relationships of any kind, and differences in parenting styles can all affect trust. Additionally, experiences and family dynamics can influence one's ability to trust. It is crucial to address these underlying issues and work together to build trust on a solid foundation. By acknowledging and discussing these challenges, you can better navigate the journey towards rebuilding trust.

Although efforts to rebuild trust can be a challenging journey, it is undoubtedly worth the effort. Each action taken to restore trust contributes to the emotional bank account of the relationship. Over time, these efforts compound, creating a stronger, more resilient bond. Rebuilding trust not only repairs the breach but also enables personal growth, intimacy, and a sense of wholeness. It is a testament to the commitment and dedication of both individuals in creating a thriving partnership.

Here are a few critical things to look for when asking for trust to be re-established.

Repentance - Authentic repentance is crucial in rebuilding trust. There must be complicity, accountability, and remorse. "I'm sorry this happened", "I take full responsibility for this happening", and "I don't ever want this to happen again" just to name a few ways communication should be experienced when offering repentance.

Transparency - 100 percent, total, unrelenting, complete transparency. Leave no area unopened because, after a breach of trust, the offended will wonder:
- "What else are you hiding from me?"
- "If you hid something from me here, how can I not believe that every other area of our marriage is not full of secrets and untruths?"

Even if there are places that are not directly related to the area of offense, do not hold back from opening up even these places. Absent the commitment to total transparency, the offended will be subject to the suggestions of their mind, which whispers "What else are they hiding?" Transparency helps to ward off unfounded thoughts of suspicion by laying bare the truth.

Honesty - Truth is a key asset in rebuilding trust. The hard facts about honesty and truth are:
1. It isn't always easy to commit to the truth
2. There can be instantaneous pain felt when being truthful

Here is the reality: the pain of truth is worth it. Any pain felt in communicating truth is short term, but the trust built will last long beyond these painful moments. Trust is very easy to lose and very hard to get back, but once you get it again, you maintain it more easily than having to rebuild it again.

Patience - Those who wish to rebuild trust must take their timetables for how long it should take and throw them out of the proverbial window. Resist the urge to ask "Are we there yet?" Commit to the work to rebuild.

Reflect on Proverbs 3:5-6: "Trust in the LORD with all your heart and lean not on your own understanding; in all your ways submit to him, and he will make your paths straight." How can trusting in God's guidance be essential in rebuilding trust in relationships?

Father, we acknowledge the importance of trust in our relationships and the challenges that come with rebuilding it. Grant us the strength to embrace repentance, transparency, and patience on this journey. May Your wisdom guide us, and may our efforts lead to healing and growth in our relationships. May Your love illuminate our path as we seek to restore and strengthen the bonds in our relationships. In Jesus' name, we pray. Amen.

REFLECTIVE APPLICATION

Take time to reflect on the areas in your relationships where trust may need to be rebuilt or strengthened. Consider how you can apply the principles of repentance, transparency, and patience to begin the journey of healing and growth.

1. Have you experienced a time where trust has been broken in your marriage? How did you deal with it? Do you feel that you are in a place where you can trust your partner now? Why or why not?

2. How can patience and a willingness work together to address the underlying issues that contribute to successfully rebuilding trust in a relationship?

DAY 7: REBUILDING TRUST: HEAL, RESTORE, AND GROW

Dear Heavenly Father, as we gather here today, we seek Your presence and guidance. We ask for Your wisdom and grace as we explore the path of rebuilding trust in relationships. May Your love and understanding fill our hearts as we embark on this journey. In Jesus' name, we pray. Amen.

Isaiah 41:10 (NIV) - "So do not fear, for I am with you; do not be dismayed, for I am your God. I will strengthen you and help you; I will uphold you with my righteous right hand."

2 Corinthians 5:18 (Good News) "God has done all this. He has restored our relationship with him through Christ, and has given us this ministry of restoring relationships."

In our previous discussions, we explored the process of rebuilding trust from the perspectives of both the offender and the offended. Today, we shift our focus to the role of the offended party in the journey of healing and restoration. The first step towards rebuilding trust as the offended party is acknowledging the pain caused by the breach of trust.

While having your trust broken was not deserved, recognizing our own imperfections and the need for grace and forgiveness is crucial to facilitating healing and restoration. By understanding and addressing our own shortcomings and embracing empathy, we not only facilitate healing for ourselves but also create an environment conducive to restoring trust in the relationship. It is important to know that those who have had much forgiven have a responsibility to forgive.

It is also important to realize that our partners, despite being good people, are susceptible to making mistakes. Just as we stand by their side when they are physically unwell, we can extend compassion and support when they are struggling emotionally, mentally, or spiritually. Recognizing their humanity allows us to approach their actions from a place of understanding rather than judgment. The oneness principle affirms this truth - if one is not well, the union is not well. It is therefore incumbent upon the one who has been offended and inflicted harm to consider ways to achieve healing for both parties with restoration as the goal.

In any relationship, forgiveness and resolving past grievances are vital. Holding onto resentment and blame will only perpetuate a cycle of pain and inhibit personal growth. While our experiences may have shaped our perceptions, seeking avenues of healing, such as personal deliverance and counseling, enables us to break free from the bondage of the past and embrace a brighter future.

It is crucial to acknowledge that the journey of rebuilding trust for the spouse who has suffered the offense can only be pursued if it is genuinely expressed and believed that the offender is repentant and willing to change course in their behavior. If we find ourselves in a cycle of neglect or abuse, it becomes imperative to prioritize our well-being and seek external help and guidance. Rebuilding trust may not be appropriate in such circumstances, and our safety should always be our top priority.

Heavenly Father, we thank You that You are the ultimate Repairer of the breech. We ask for Your wisdom and guidance as we seek to rebuild trust in areas of our marriage that have been broken and mishandled. May the words shared today serve as a source of hope and encouragement for those on this journey. We lift our marriage and all marriages for those seeking to restore trust in their relationship. Help us to embody the qualities of love and grace as we move forward in life together. In Jesus' name, we pray. Amen.

REFLECTIVE APPLICATION

Consider how embracing forgiveness, understanding the humanity of others, and nurturing trust align with the promise in Isaiah 41:10. Reflect on how God's strength and presence can uphold you as you embark on the journey of healing and rebuilding trust in your relationships.

1. How can you apply the principles of forgiveness and empathy in your relationships?

2. What shared mission or goal can you establish with your partner or loved one to strengthen your connection?

DAY 8: COMMUNICATION THAT CONNECTS

Dear Lord, we come before you with grateful hearts, thankful for the ability to share moments with each other that helps to deepen our connection. Let our conversation and communication with each other supercede the mundane activities of our day. Instead let us enjoy moments of vulnerability, shared experiences and laughter.

Ephesians 4:29 (NLT) -"Don't use foul or abusive language. Let everything you say be good and helpful, so that your words will be an encouragement to those who hear them."

Proverbs 18:13 (NIV) "To answer before listening—that is folly and shame."

Couples who have been married for some time can find themselves engaging in routine conversations about the mundane more often than they would desire. The daily grind of household management tasks, caring for children, managing extracurriculars, fighting unrelenting traffic, and dealing with work and its stresses, all to do it again the next day, can consume conversations between spouses. If we are not careful, the exciting conversation offered when we were learning each other can give way to surface-level communications that address tasks more than our need for a common connection.

As couples live together in marriage through many seasons, it is important to focus on communication that connects. Beyond the mundane and routine, couples are greatly served when they can leverage and make space for communication that allows for introspection and reflection, hope and future thinking, as well as optimism and dream casting. This is an important item to focus on because of this fact: time brings opportunities for change. Change in marriage is inevitable, and healthy marriages evolve as they undergo the various seasons of life. As this evolution happens, couples who can communicate about the changes they undergo give new life to conversations that were once monotonous and bland.

One way to do this is to share moments of the day and how those moments had an impact on you both. This exercise goes beyond recounting the facts of the routine happenings of the day and reveals how those events made us feel. Try sharing a funny moment, or even an awkward moment, from your day with your spouse. Awkward situations are an inevitable part of life, occurring at the most unexpected moments, and sometimes leaving us cringing with embarrassment. We all experience awkward moments, those cringe-worthy instances that make us want to disappear into thin air. The ability to share these moments with your spouse and perhaps even share laughter about them together can help to keep things light and fun. Keep in mind that communication does not always have to be arduous. Additionally, communication is the vehicle that allows you both to continue to learn about each other. Never underestimate the power of not taking each other too seriously all the time. Find ways to laugh together, leverage quirky moments, and be friends.

Heavenly Father, we thank You for the ability to effectively communicate with one another. We thank you for the gift of humor and shared laughter. Help us embrace life's quirks and the sometimes awkward moments we find ourselves in with a merry heart and disposition. May we find joy in the humorous side of our everyday interactions and create bonds of laughter with each other and those around us. Fill us with Your joy. In Your name, we pray. Amen.

REFLECTIVE APPLICATION

Share a lighthearted, awkward moment or embarrassing story with your spouse. Embrace the humor in the situation and encourage laughter as you relive the memory together. Consider how these shared moments strengthen your bond and bring joy into your relationship.

1. Can you recall a hilariously awkward encounter from your own life? How did you handle it, and what did you learn from it? Share this encounter with your spouse.

2. How does humor and shared laughter help build stronger connections and relationships with each other?

DAY 9: YOUR MARRIAGE NEEDS COMMUNITY

Heavenly Father, we come before You with gratitude for the gift of community and the support it provides in our lives. As we explore the impact of community in marriages, may Your wisdom and love guide us in choosing our own healthy community that promotes the health of and longevity of our marriage. Amen.

Ecclesiastes 4:9-10 (NIV) - "Two are better than one, because they have a good return for their labor: If either of them falls down, one can help the other up. But pity anyone who falls and has no one to help them up."

Geoff

In a world where individualism often dominates, it's important to recognize the profound impact that community can have on our lives. Today, we will explore how a supportive community can contribute to the strength and longevity of a relationship. Join us on day 9 as we delve into the power of having a strong and supportive community on your marriage journey.

Community, in the context of marriage, extends beyond immediate family and neighbors. It encompasses a network of relationships that provide a sense of belonging, support, and guidance. These connections are crucial for married couples as they offer a shared space for growth and understanding. A strong community reminds couples they are not alone in their journey, and that others have walked similar paths before them.

At the core of our story, we have been fortunate enough to be surrounded by a community that embraces and uplifts us. Our friends and family see us as one, providing unwavering support, even during our lowest moments. Having genuine connections can help propel a couple forward, enabling them to weather the storms that life throws their way.

Among the pillars of support in our lives are grandparents, particularly our grandmothers. These individuals (affectionately known as Gram and Granny) symbolize the strength and resilience that comes from having a community that genuinely cares. Their presence, along with the unwavering support of others in our family and extended family, reminds us of the strong familial bonds within our community. Jasmine and I have been fortunate to share close bonds with other couples who have become our trusted confidants, travel companions, and safe spaces. Every couple needs a safe space to share freely and openly without judgment, sabotage, or the fear that their personal business will be weaponized against them.

Our story is a beautiful testament to the transformative power of community within marriages. Through the consistent support of loved ones, friends, and even those admired from afar, couples can find strength, support, and encouragement. The sense of oneness that comes from being part of a community enriches lives and fosters personal growth. Let this heartwarming entry inspire you to cherish and cultivate your communities that are advocates of your marriage, for they hold the potential to uplift and empower us in ways we may never achieve alone.

Reflect on Ecclesiastes 4:9-10: "Two are better than one, because they have a good return for their labor: If either of them falls down, one can help the other up. But pity anyone who falls and has no one to help them up." How does this verse emphasize the importance of community and support in marriage?

Heavenly Father, we thank You for the gift of community and the strength it provides to marriages. May we cherish the bonds we share with others and seek to uplift and support one another. Guide us to be active members of our communities and bless our marriages through these connections. In Jesus' name, we pray. Amen.

REFLECTIVE APPLICATION

Reach out to someone in your community, whether a friend, family member, or mentor, and express your appreciation for their support and presence in your life. Reflect on how these connections have influenced your relationships.

1. How has your community, whether it be friends, family, or mentors, impacted your marriage or relationships?

2. Can you think of a specific instance where the support of your community helped you navigate a challenging time in your relationship? How did it make a difference?

DAY 10: A LIFETIME OF COMMITMENT: INSIGHTS FROM A 63-YEAR MARRIAGE

Heavenly Father, we thank You for the example of enduring commitment and love that Bill and Dorothy Vaught have set through their 63-year marriage. As we explore their journey and insight, may we find wisdom and inspiration to strengthen our own relationships. In Jesus' name, we pray, Amen.

1 Corinthians 13:4-7 (NIV) - "Love is patient, love is kind. It does not envy, it does not boast, it is not proud. It does not dishonor others, it is not self-seeking, it is not easily angered, it keeps no record of wrongs. Love does not delight in evil but rejoices with the truth. It always protects, always trusts, always hopes, always perseveres."

Jasmine

A few years ago, Geoff and I had the privilege to sit down and have a recorded conversation with my grandparents- William "Bill" and Dorothy "Dot" Vaught. At that time, they had been married for 63 years. They met in 7th grade. Sadly in 2021, they both passed away and departed this life only 8 days apart from one another. They had just celebrated their 66th wedding anniversary on October 5th. My grandmother transitioned on October 12th, and then my grandfather on October 20th. My grandfather watched as my grandmother took her last breaths. When he later ended up in the hospital a few days after her passing, the doctor caring for him told my mother that he had "suffered trauma to the heart" when referring to my grandfather's condition. When I arrived at my grandfather's bedside a day later, he told me that he didn't want to be here without her, referring to my Gram, his wife. Only 2 days later, as I sat by his bedside holding his hand, he slept away into eternity.

Their love left an everlasting imprint on me. Not just me but everyone who knew and had encountered them and their testimony. It was a love fortified by a strong commitment to one another, no matter what obstacles they faced in life. Whatever those obstacles were, they were determined to face them together- and did. Their example continues to resonate with me in my own marriage to this day. I want that same kind of commitment and endurance that says no matter what we face, we will do it together. For them, it was even in death. Isn't that what we all want: a committed love that will withstand the test of time?

Marriage is an intricate journey, filled with both joys and challenges. In a world where divorce rates are soaring, it is truly remarkable to have grandparents like Bill and Dorothy Vaught. Their enduring relationship is a testament to the commitment, dedication, and support required to make a marriage last. Today, we will share key lessons they learned throughout their 66-year journey together.

Bill and Dorothy's love story began in school: they first met in the 7th grade and married after high school. Their initial connection was rooted in admiration for each other's qualities, such as Dorothy's kindness and Bill's calm demeanor. A vital aspect of their enduring marriage was the commitment they made to God and each other. Dorothy recognized the need to strengthen her relationship with the Lord, which ultimately strengthened her bond with Bill. With their unwavering commitment throughout the difficulties they experienced, Dorothy sought solace in prayer and the support of like-minded women devoted to interceding for their marriages.

My grandparents' marriage had its fair share of hard times and challenges. Early on in their marriage, my grandfather Bill battled an alcohol addiction that brought him very near to death. Oftentimes, this left my grandmother to bear the weight of responsibility in the household, including taking care of my mom by herself. My grandmother Dorothy did not relent in her belief that God would deliver and set my grandfather free. Through the power of God, fervent prayer and determination, my grandfather broke free from his alcohol addiction and lived over 50 years sober until the day of his passing. As his granddaughter, I never knew him NOT sober.

My grandmother, Dorothy had an relentless commitment to her vows and the faith that helped her stay strong throughout the difficult seasons. During our conversation a few years ago, she vividly recalled the echoes of her wedding vows in her mind during difficult times, reminding her of the promises she had made to God and her husband, Bill. Rather than running from their problems, she sought great solace in her prayer life, finding the strength to face adversity head-on. As a personal testimony, I had the benefit of being raised in the home with them. I saw firsthand the gift of their love for one another. Over the years, my grandfather faced several serious health challenges, and my grandmother never left his side.

Another major lesson my grandparents shared is the importance of supporting and appreciating one another. My grandmother, Dorothy, highlighted my grandfather's consistent support and belief in her abilities. He allowed her to be herself and to live a life of service to others. Throughout the conversation, my grandfather, Bill, acknowledged my grandmother's kind-heartedness and willingness to lend a helping hand. By allowing each other to be their authentic selves and supporting one another through thick and thin, their marriage thrived when it could have died.

Reflecting on the wisdom shared by my grandparents' example, it becomes evident that a successful marriage requires three major components: unwavering commitment, dedication, and support for one another. Bill and Dorothy's story serves as an inspiration for couples to face the challenges in their own relationship together. By prioritizing their vows, relying on their faith, and appreciating each other's unique qualities, the Vaughts created a lasting and loving marriage that extended beyond them into a family legacy of love. Their journey teaches us that with love, commitment, and a strong foundation, a lifetime of happiness and fulfillment is possible.

Reflect on 1 Corinthians 13:4-7: "Love is patient, love is kind. It does not envy, it does not boast, it is not proud. It does not dishonor others, it is not self-seeking, it is not easily angered, it keeps no record of wrongs. Love does not delight in evil but rejoices with the truth. It always protects, always trusts, always hopes, always perseveres." How do these verses resonate with the enduring love and commitment of Bill and Dorothy Vaught?

Heavenly Father, we thank You for the enduring love and commitment displayed by Bill and Dorothy Vaught in their 66-year marriage. May their story inspire us to prioritize our vows, rely on our faith, and appreciate the unique qualities of our partners. Guide us in strengthening our relationships through unwavering commitment, dedication, and support. In Jesus' name, we pray. Amen.

REFLECTIVE APPLICATION

Take some time to reflect on your own vows or commitments in your marriage. Consider how you can strengthen your bond by prioritizing these promises and supporting one another.

1. What aspects of Bill and Dorothy Vaught's marriage story resonate with you the most?

2. How can you apply the lessons of commitment, faith, and mutual support to your own relationship or marriage?

_____
_____
_____
_____
_____
_____
_____
_____
_____
_____
_____
_____
_____
_____
_____
_____
_____
_____
_____
_____
_____
_____
_____
_____
_____
_____
_____
_____

DAY 11: BUILDING ON A FIRM FOUNDATION

Heavenly Father, as we journey through the complexities of marriage, we seek Your guidance and strength. Help us embrace the art of renovation as we build on a firm foundation of love, commitment, and growth. Amen.

Ephesians 4:32 (NIV) - "Be kind and compassionate to one another, forgiving each other, just as in Christ God forgave you."

As we navigate this lifelong adventure called marriage, we must recognize the need for ongoing maintenance and, sometimes, renovation. This commitment to marital reflection and rebuilding allows us to have the courage to continually build on a firm foundation as the seasons of life change and shift.

One fundamental truth highlighted in this conversation is the danger of succumbing to external expectations in a marriage. The term "external expectations" in marriage refers to the perspectives, expectations, and opinions of those outside the union. The essence of a successful marriage lies in the unique dynamics between the couple involved. By placing external expectations of marriage within its proper context, we can relate to one another authentically. Authenticity serves as the breeding ground for vulnerability, intimacy, and trust. Embracing authenticity allows couples to build a sturdy foundation that can withstand the challenges of different seasons.

Recognizing the areas in need of renovation is a crucial step in nurturing a healthy relationship. Whether it is communication, trust, managing finances, parenting, or other external factors, acknowledging flaws and unique challenges in your union is the first step toward growth. To do this, we must confront these issues honestly. Seeking guidance from others who can be trusted (i.e. those who have successfully faced similar struggles), facilitating healing through professional counseling, and engaging in difficult conversations are all helpful options to build a sustainably healthy union during the ebbs and flows of life. It is important, however, to remember that each marriage is unique, and the renovation process must be approached with an open mind and heart.

Renovating your marriage is not something to fear, nor should it be viewed as a sign of failure. It requires courage and a willingness to step into the unknown. Seeking help or guidance, and approaching the process with curiosity are essential. While not all spouses may be equally open to change, perseverance and support are key. Together, as a married couple, you can keep building the marriage God joined together.

Reflect on Ephesians 4:32: "Be kind and compassionate to one another, forgiving each other, just as in Christ God forgave you." How does this scripture guide us in the renovation of our marriages?

Dear Lord, we pray for the courage to embrace the art of renovation in our marriages. Allow us to not get stuck dwelling on past mistakes and missteps. Help us not to be afraid to begin again, when needed, in our building process. May we be kind, compassionate, and forgiving, just as You have forgiven us. Guide us as we build on a firm foundation of love and commitment. We thank You for the opportunity to grow and strengthen our marriages through renovation. Grant us the courage and wisdom to build on a firm foundation of love and commitment. In Jesus' name, we pray. Amen.

REFLECTIVE APPLICATION

Take time to have an open and honest conversation with your spouse about areas in your relationship that may need improvement. Share your feelings, concerns, and hopes for the future. Discuss potential steps you can take together to work on these areas.

1. Reflect on a time when authenticity and vulnerability strengthened your relationship. How did it impact your connection with your spouse or partner?

2. Consider the areas in your marriage that may need renovation. How can you take the first step toward addressing these challenges honestly and openly?

_____
_____
_____
_____
_____
_____
_____
_____
_____
_____
_____
_____
_____
_____
_____
_____
_____
_____
_____
_____
_____
_____
_____
_____
_____
_____
_____

DAY 12: THE ART OF FIGHTING FAIR

Gracious Father, as we explore the art of fighting fair in our relationships, we seek Your wisdom and guidance. Help us approach conflict with love, respect, and a commitment to growth. Amen.

Proverbs 15:1 (NIV) - "A gentle answer turns away wrath, but a harsh word stirs up anger."

Conflict is an inevitable part of any relationship, but how we handle these conflicts truly defines the strength and longevity of our bond. How we handle conflict in our marriage can reveal much about who we are. It can tell the story of our past traumas and present realities in our relationship. As a couple, we have had our fair share of conflicts that led to verbal fights! It has required deep and intentional work to learn the "art of fighting fair." At times, we have gotten things right, and, at other times, we have gotten things really wrong. We would be liars if we said we are masters of this topic, but we have spent a great deal of time putting in the work to avoid the damage to our relationship that comes when we do not fight fair. We hope and pray that you can avoid some of the damaging mistakes we have made on our journey to learn the art of fighting fair.

On day 12, we emphasize the importance of recognizing conflict as an opportunity for communication, rather than a battleground. Conflicts should never turn into personal attacks, as the ultimate goal should be to understand, not harm. Disagreements can lead to growth and restoration when handled with care and respect.

In our journey, we have learned to set realistic expectations about conflicts in our marriage. Conflict is not inherently detrimental, and avoiding it can hinder growth. By approaching conflicts with the right mindset, you can discover that conflicts become opportunities for strengthening your bond.

We highlight the need to avoid extreme language and terms during conflicts. Words like "always" and "never" can be alienating and prevent resolution. We caution against bringing up past issues or making sweeping statements, which undermine the chances of finding a resolution. Staying focused on the present moment is key.

To foster constructive conflict resolution, we emphasize the importance of staying in the present moment. We'd like to share the "parking lot" technique, which allows certain aspects of the conflict to be temporarily set aside, or parked, to keep the conversation focused on the main issue. This approach ensures that unrelated issues do not derail the resolution process.

We firmly believe that conflicts should be faced head-on. We encourage open and honest conversations, even when they become intense. However, be open to reconciliation after a conflict. Remember that conflicts are opportunities for growth and a chance to fight as a team against anything threatening your unity. Remember that your partner is not your enemy. Satan is the adversary of your souls; he is your common enemy, and he hates covenant and marriage. There will always be opposition against your marriage that you will have to guard and fight against. However, your partner should not be considered your opponent, but your teammate in this fight.

Reflect on Proverbs 15:1: "A gentle answer turns away wrath, but a harsh word stirs up anger." How can this verse guide us in constructively fighting fairly and resolving conflicts?

Reflect on Ephesians 6:11-12: "Put on all of God's armor so that you will be able to stand firm against the strategies of the devil. For we are not fighting against flesh and blood enemies, but against evil rulers and authorities of the unseen world, against mighty powers in this dark world, and against evil spirits in heavenly places."

Dear Lord, grant us the wisdom to fight fair in our relationships. May we approach conflicts with love, respect, and a commitment to growth. Help us remember that conflicts are opportunities for understanding each other and strengthening our bonds. Help us apply these principles in our relationships so we can grow and bring you glory in our marriage. We pray that you give us wisdom and discernment to handle each other graciously and lovingly during conflict. In Jesus' name we pray, Amen.

REFLECTIVE APPLICATION

Take time to discuss the concept of fighting fairly with your spouse. Share your thoughts and feelings about how conflicts are approached in your relationship. Identify specific areas where you can improve in handling conflicts constructively.

1. Think of a recent conflict you've experienced in your relationship. How could the principles of "fighting fair" have improved the resolution of that conflict?

2. Reflect on Proverbs 15:1. How can you apply the principle of a "gentle answer" in your conflicts and disagreements

3. Discuss Ephesians 6:11-12. How can you both be more vigilant to guard against the devices of Satan, specifically in the area of conflict?

_____
_____
_____
_____
_____
_____
_____
_____
_____
_____
_____
_____
_____
_____
_____
_____
_____
_____
_____
_____
_____
_____
_____

DAY 13: LOVE HAS A LANGUAGE

Father God, we come before You today with gratitude for the gift of love and the opportunity to grow closer in our relationships. As we explore the concept of love languages, may Your wisdom guide us in understanding and connecting with our partners on a deeper level. In Jesus' name, we pray. Amen

Song of Solomon 7:10 (NIV) "I belong to my beloved, and his desire is for me."

Love is a universal language, but did you know we all have different ways of expressing and receiving love? In his book, "The Five Love Languages," Dr. Gary Chapman explores the concept that understanding our partner's primary love language can significantly improve communication and strengthen relationships. Understanding how your partner receives and gives love can have a lasting impact on your relationship that promotes intimacy and a deeper awareness of one another's needs. Love languages are unique ways in which individuals express and interpret love. The five love languages, as outlined by Gary Chapman, are acts of service, physical touch, quality time, words of affirmation, and giving and receiving gifts. Each person has a way that they best receive love, which determines how they feel most loved and appreciated. By identifying and understanding your partner's love language(s), you can effectively communicate your affection and ensure your gestures resonate deeply with them.

It is common for couples to experience frustration and resentment when they are not in tune with how each other receives their language of love and appreciation. For instance, imagine a spouse feels most loved when spending quality time with her partner. Her partner enjoys buying her gifts and sees this as a way to express love and never makes quality time a priority. This could leave them both with feelings of unappreciation for the other. To the spouse buying gifts, it can feel like his spouse is not appreciative of his efforts to express love. The wife can feel unsatisfied and even worse, unseen. This miscommunication of love language can result in unmet expectations. By being aware of, recognizing, and appreciating each other's differences and needs, couples can avoid unnecessary conflicts and deepen their emotional connection. The goal should be to align your actions with your partner's love language(s), making them feel cherished, known, and understood.

Discovering your own love language(s), and that of your partner, can be an enlightening experience. To assist in this process, Gary Chapman's website offers a simple online test that helps identify your primary love language(s). The test provides valuable insights into how you prefer to give and receive love, allowing you to better understand yourself and your partner. It is important to note that love languages can evolve, as growth and evolution should be expected. Staying attuned to each other's changing needs is crucial for continued relationship growth and the ability to love each other as you evolve.

Once you have identified your love languages, it is essential to communicate them to your partner openly. By expressing your preferences and explaining how you interpret love, you enable your partner to fulfill your emotional needs more effectively. Open and honest communication about your love languages fosters understanding and empathy, creating a stronger foundation for your relationship. Remember, love languages are not a one-size-fits-all solution, but rather a tool to enhance connection and intimacy. It is crucial to remain patient and committed to learning and practicing each other's languages of love. Relationships require effort, compromise, and understanding. Give each other space to evolve, and pay attention to each other's needs, as your language may change over time. Knowing your partner's love language is an ongoing process. By dedicating yourself to speaking each other's love languages, you can create a harmonious and fulfilling relationship built on mutual respect, appreciation, and affection. Understanding and embracing the concept of love languages can revolutionize how you communicate love in your relationship. By identifying and aligning with your partner's primary love language, you can cultivate a deeper emotional connection and avoid unnecessary conflicts.

Remember, love languages are not fixed but can evolve, so keep the lines of communication open and be willing to adapt. Be intentional about paying attention to each other's needs, as those needs will evolve and change with the seasons of your marriage. By embracing this knowledge and applying it in your relationship, you can create a love that speaks directly to your partner's heart.

Lord, grant us the patience, kindness, and understanding needed to navigate our differences and to speak each other's language of love fluently. Help us to remember that our love should be a reflection of Your divine love for us. Bless our marriage with a love that lasts and endures throughout all seasons. May we commit our marriage into Your loving and capable hands, trusting that You will guide us as we grow in love and unity. In Jesus' name, we pray. Amen.

REFLECTIVE APPLICATION

1. What steps can you take to ensure that your dedication to understanding and practicing each other's love languages remains unwavering?

2. Share a personal experience where patience and dedication to your partner's love language resulted in a stronger and more loving interaction between you.

DAY 14: NAVIGATING THE CHALLENGES OF MARRIAGE (THE HUSBAND'S PERSPECTIVE)

Dear Lord, we come before You seeking wisdom and understanding as we explore the challenges faced by husbands in marriage. May today's devotion shed light on managing the complexities of married life and provide valuable insights for those faithfully on this journey. Amen.

Ephesians 5:25-29 (NKJV)-
"Husbands, love your wives, just as Christ also loved the church and gave Himself for her, that He might sanctify and cleanse her with the washing of water by the word, that He might present her to Himself a glorious church, not having spot or wrinkle or any such thing, but that she should be holy and without blemish. So husbands ought to love their own wives as their own bodies; he who loves his wife loves himself. For no one ever hated his own flesh, but nourishes and cherishes it, just as the Lord does the church."

Geoff

Various aspects can make it challenging for husbands to fulfill their roles in marriage. Challenges that range from a lack of forgiveness to ineffective communication. One of the recurring themes that emerges is the importance of patience in a marriage. There are times when your wife's lack of patience can sometimes make it difficult for you to be the husband you aspire to be. While recognizing that no relationship can be perfect, the significance of having a partner who believes in the strength of your bond, even during challenging moments is key. This reflection highlights the need for understanding and compassion within a marriage.

Some husbands may struggle with harnessing language that reveals their hearts when communicating in marriage. This struggle is especially evident when navigating conflict. Differences in communication styles can make authentic communication feel nearly impossible. In marriage, our words hold immense power, both in building your home and potentially tearing it down. To understand the weight of language, you need grace and forgiveness when words fail to align with intentions. Through time, you both can grow in your ability to express yourselves effectively, using words that bring growth and understanding, rather than harm.

Patience is also critical when evaluating the successes and failures of marriage. Most marriages will evolve, and no marriage begins fully formed into what it was intended to be. Well-balanced perspectives on the growth track and progress of marriage can be found through seeking support from other men who value God-honoring marriages. There is safety in finding a trustworthy confidant with whom you can share the trials and tribulations of married life. This camaraderie allows husbands to realize that they are not alone in their struggles and can draw strength from the shared experiences of others. It also provides a platform for encouragement and growth, as iron sharpens iron.

Reflect on Ecclesiastes 4:9-10: "Two are better than one, because they have a good return for their labor: If either of them falls down, one can help the other up. But pity anyone who falls and has no one to help them up." How does this verse emphasize the importance of support and companionship in marriage, especially during challenging times?

Heavenly Father, we thank You for the wisdom You give us in navigating the challenges husbands face in marriage. May these insights serve as a source of encouragement and guidance for those navigating the complexities of married life. Help us to remember that we are not alone in our struggles and that through patience, grace, and support, we can strengthen our marriages. In Jesus' name, we pray. Amen.

REFLECTIVE APPLICATION

If you have a relationship with a fellow trusted husband, reach out to him and engage in a candid conversation about the challenges and joys of marriage. Share insights, offer support, and encourage one another on your respective journeys. Reflect on how these conversations can strengthen your relationships and provide valuable perspectives.

1. How has patience played a role in your own marriage or relationships? How do you navigate challenging moments with patience and understanding?

2. Can you think of a time when words and communication had a significant impact on your relationship? How did you work through it, and what did you learn from the experience?

3. Consider the importance of seeking support from a community of like-minded individuals in your marriage or relationships. How has this support influenced your journey?

DAY 15: NAVIGATING IDENTITY AND EXPECTATIONS IN MARRIAGE (THE WIFE'S PERSPECTIVE)

Dear Lord, we come before You seeking wisdom and guidance as we explore the complexities of identity and expectations in marriage. May Your light shine upon our understanding, and may we approach this topic with open hearts and minds. Amen.

Ephesians 5:31-32 (NIV) - "For this reason, a man will leave his father and mother and be united to his wife, and the two will become one flesh. This is a profound mystery—but I am talking about Christ and the church."

Proverbs 12:4 (NLT)- "A worthy wife is a crown for her husband, but a disgraceful woman is like cancer in his bones."

Jasmine

At the beginning of my marriage, I was so excited and happy to be my husband's wife. For context, growing up I always knew that I wanted to be a mother, but I was not fixated on becoming a wife. I didn't grow up with aspirations to be a bride and have a big wedding as most little girls do. I did not aspire to be anyone's wife. To be fully transparent, I had doubts about truly finding someone who would love me for me entirely, and I knew I would be unwilling to settle for anything that made me feel less.

Enter my husband, who worked hard to gain my trust and security in his intentions and feelings for me. Although reluctant to be hurt, I quickly fell in love with my husband. I knew that I did not want to spend the rest of my life apart from him. That was when the desire to become HIS wife became a reality. When we married, I fell headfirst into my role, duties, and responsibilities of what I believed a wife should be. Ensuring I was a "good wife" to my husband was the goal and priority.

By our first wedding anniversary, I was 5 months pregnant with our first child. Once our firstborn came along at almost 10 weeks premature, I was thrust into my next role as a mother. It did not take very long after the first 2-3 years of our marriage to realize that I had lost my sense of self. My identity had morphed into being what my family needed me to be whenever they needed me to be it. It was what I knew to do because this is what I grew up seeing. My mom and grandmother both sacrificed their lives for their family. They embodied the spirit of humility and selflessness many times at their own expense. As a wife and or mother, it is easy to become so preoccupied with the needs of those you serve and care for that you neglect your sense of self. Ultimately, I had to re-submit that part of me to God and ask Him to redefine the identity that He had in mind for me in my evolution to becoming a wife and mother. I will tell you that the redefinition of my identity is still something I constantly seek God about as the seasons change in my life. I don't want to settle or rely on my own thoughts and feelings about it, so I find safety in entrusting that part of me to my Father and not external entities.

In today's rapidly evolving society, the concept of marriage and the roles within it have undergone significant changes. As you and your spouse explore the topic of identity and expectations in marriage, it is important to approach the subject with an open mind and acknowledge the diverse experiences and perspectives of each individual. There are specific complexities that wives often face, particularly concerning societal expectations and personal growth. Wives can find themselves grappling with societal expectations, influenced by cultural norms, religious beliefs, and the influence of popular women's empowerment movements over time. Some messages can be conflicting, leaving wives to question their roles and responsibilities in their union.

The concept of submission, for instance, can be complex to navigate, especially for wives. Submission has often been used as an oppressive tool in the conversation of marriage. The scripture in Ephesians 5:22 says, "For wives, this means submit to your husbands as to the Lord." Ephesians 5:21 in The New Living Translation offers a nuance "And further, submit to one another out of reverence for Christ." This scripture promotes that there is a mutual submission that occurs in marriage. When my husband and I counsel couples we spend time discussing the meaning of. "Mutual submission." One of the things we encourage couples to do is to consider and develop a common mission for their marriage and to ensure that all decisions and actions "come under" and are subject to that mission, hence - submission.

It is critical to remember that each couple's interpretation and practice of submission may differ, and it is an ongoing conversation that requires open communication and mutual understanding between partners.

The journey towards oneness in your marriage does not negate your personal self-discovery as a wife. The pressure to conform to societal standards and the fear of judgment can create a sense of insecurity. Wives need to realize that authenticity does not mean abandoning their roles as wives, but rather embracing their unique strengths and interests, in addition to their role as wives. Embracing one's awareness of self, without losing sight of the connection and collaboration with their spouse, is essential for building your marriage. As wives, we must resist the urge to compare ourselves, and our relationships with our husbands, to other marriages around us. Comparing oneself to others can rob joy and hinder growth for both you and your husband.

Finally, communication is essential in any relationship, especially in your marriage. Couples must engage in open and honest conversations about their evolving identity, expectations, aspirations, and needs. Sharing personal journeys and discussing individual growth within the context of the marriage fosters understanding and strengthens the bond between partners.

Both spouses must support each other's personal growth and encourage the pursuit of individual interests and passions.

Reflect on the concept of unity and oneness in marriage as discussed in Ephesians 5:21-22 and Ephesians 5:31-32. How can a husband and wife work together to achieve unity while still celebrating and respecting each other's individual identities and aspirations?

Heavenly Father, we thank You for making us unique by personal design. You are a good Father and You are aware of our need for increased wisdom in the area of our exploration of identity and expectations in marriage. May these insights serve as a source of encouragement and guidance for those navigating the complexities of married life. Help us approach marriage with open hearts and open minds, embracing unity and mutual submission within the sacred bond of matrimony. If there is presently a wife struggling in the area of identity, expectations, or purpose, we ask that You come into their situation and bring clarity, direction, and peace. In Jesus' name, Amen.

REFLECTIVE APPLICATION

Engage in a heartfelt conversation with your spouse or partner about your individual identities and aspirations within the context of your relationship. Share your personal journeys and discuss how you can support each other's growth and authenticity while maintaining a strong bond. Reflect on how this open dialogue can strengthen your connection and understanding as a couple.

1. How have societal expectations influenced your perceptions of roles and identity within marriage or relationships?

2. Can you relate to the struggle of navigating personal growth and authenticity with the expectations placed on you as a spouse? How have you approached this challenge?

DAY 16: NURTURING INTIMACY IN MARRIAGE

Dear Lord, we come before You seeking understanding and guidance as we explore the multifaceted nature of intimacy in marriage. May Your wisdom and guidance be upon us as we reflect on the importance of both physical and non-physical intimacy in the sacred bond of matrimony. In Jesus' name, Amen.

1 Corinthians 7:3-5 (NIV) - "The husband should fulfill his marital duty to his wife, and likewise the wife to her husband. The wife does not have authority over her own body but yields it to her husband. In the same way, the husband does not have authority over his own body but yields it to his wife. Do not deprive each other except perhaps by mutual consent and for a time, so that you may devote yourselves to prayer. Then come together again so that Satan will not tempt you because of your lack of self-control."

Intimacy is often limited to being synonymous with sex. Although sex is absolutely meaningful and necessary in how we should express our love and desire for each other, intimacy involves so much more than sex alone. It is essential to recognize that within the realm of marriage, both physical and non-physical intimacy play a significant role in fostering a deep and fulfilling connection. It involves any physical act of connection, such as hugging, kissing, or even a simple touch. In addition to physical touch, intimacy also encompasses meeting emotional and mental needs in the relationship. It is the merging of the material and non-material elements, creating a sacred space that defines the unique bond between a couple.

Intimacy is foundational in a marriage. It fosters vulnerability and accountability, strengthening the bond between partners. It is through intimacy that couples build closeness, trust, and understanding. The sacred space created by intimacy is exclusive to the couple, setting their relationship apart from any other. This sense of exclusivity enhances the connection between partners, allowing them to communicate and articulate their needs in ways that words alone cannot express.

Reflect on the concept of vulnerability within your marriage. How does vulnerability facilitate intimacy, and why is this openness important for the health of your marital relationship?

Whether it be third-party involvement, financial dependencies, or even violations of personal boundaries, breaches of this vulnerability can erode trust and intimacy. To rebuild intimacy, it is crucial to remove any external factors that have infiltrated the sacred space of the relationship. Establishing and reinforcing boundaries are essential to protect intimacy from future breaches.

Think about the concept of boundaries in marriage. How can boundaries help protect and preserve the intimacy of the marital relationship? Are there areas where boundaries may need to be established or reinforced in your marriage?

While physical intimacy may face obstacles due to medical issues, medication, or impotence, it is important to remember that intimacy extends beyond the act of intercourse. Couples should explore alternative ways to foster intimacy, focusing on emotional and mental connections. Communication is key in navigating these challenges, allowing partners to express their needs, desires, and insecurities openly. By understanding and supporting each other, you can maintain and nurture intimacy, even in the face of physical limitations.

Nurturing intimacy within marriage is a lifelong journey that requires dedication, trust, and open communication. It is a multifaceted concept that encompasses physical, emotional, mental, and spiritual connections. While external factors and experiences can challenge intimacy, this sacred space can be rebuilt through open communication, establishing boundaries, and prioritizing the unique bond between partners. By nurturing intimacy, couples can strengthen their relationship, experience a deeper level of connection, and enjoy the benefits it brings to their marriage.

Consider 1 Corinthians 7:3-5, which emphasizes the importance of fulfilling one another's marital duties. How does this passage highlight the significance of physical intimacy in marriage? How can physical intimacy be a reflection of the deeper emotional and spiritual connection between spouses?

Heavenly Father, Help us to build marriages that reflect Your love and grace. May our relationships be a testament to Your faithfulness and transformative power. Lord, help us to understand and speak each other's love languages fluently, so we may communicate love more effectively. In Jesus' name we pray, Amen.

REFLECTIVE APPLICATION

Engage in a conversation with your spouse about the different dimensions of intimacy in your relationship. Discuss what aspects of intimacy are most meaningful to each of you and explore ways to nurture and strengthen those connections. Additionally, consider any challenges you may have faced or are currently facing with intimacy, and brainstorm strategies for overcoming them together.

1. How do you define intimacy within the context of your marriage or relationship? What aspects of intimacy are most important to you and your partner?

2. Have you and your spouse faced challenges to intimacy, whether external factors or physical limitations? How have you navigated these challenges together?

DAY 17: MARRIAGE AND MINISTRY: A JOURNEY OF LOVE AND SERVICE

Dear Heavenly Father, we come before You with gratitude for the love and dedication of couples who serve in ministry together. As we explore the challenges and blessings of balancing marriage and ministry, may Your wisdom and guidance be with us. Bless these couples and their unique journeys of love and service. Amen.

Genesis 2:18 (NLT)- "Then the Lord God said, "It is not good for the man to be alone. I will make a helper who is just right for him."

The sacred union of two hearts joining together to become one is a complex odyssey in and of itself. When you couple that with being in ministry together, it adds a layer of intense focus and attention. Often, we hear stories from the perspective of men in ministry, but it is equally important to listen to the experiences of wives who walk alongside their husbands on this path. It is not an easy journey, as it requires navigating the complexities of being a spouse, a parent, and a partner in ministry. It's important to note that marriage itself is a ministry. However, there can be an additional demand on a marriage when a husband and wife carry the weight of serving in a ministry together. Today we will explore insights for marriage within the context of those who serve together in ministry. Our objective is to gain a deeper understanding of the delicate balance needed to successfully be present in both marriage and ministry.

For many wives, being married is already a significant responsibility in itself. Learning how to be a supportive partner and understanding the needs of one's spouse can be a lifelong journey. But when ministry enters the equation, the dynamics can quickly change. Some couples may even work together in business ventures, and, while it may not be the same as ministry, it presents its own set of similar challenges. A wife's desire to walk beside her husband in ministry is a unique calling, and it is important to acknowledge and appreciate the women who embrace this role with clarity and courage.

Women who work with their spouses in ministry must acknowledge that their assignment and calling is not something their husbands have given them or defined for them. Rather, it is a calling they feel deeply within themselves from God. These women have an independent sense of purpose and a profound understanding that they have a role to fulfill alongside their husbands. The blessing lies in how ministry partners naturally connect, allowing them to complement and support one another in their respective ministries. This recognition brings strength and resilience to their relationship, enabling them to navigate the challenges that can arise.

Maintaining a healthy tension between marriage, ministry, and other responsibilities is no easy task. The demands of life, children, jobs, and ministry can easily become overwhelming. Boundaries become crucial in creating a space for a couple to thrive. These boundaries can include intentionally setting aside time to focus on each other and not allowing ministry discussions to dominate their conversations. It is important to find moments of joy, laughter, and relaxation amidst the demands of their shared responsibilities.

Communication and reliance on the Holy Spirit as the leader play vital roles in successfully navigating the complexities of marriage and ministry. Effective communication ensures that both partners feel heard and understood, fostering a sense of unity. Additionally, seeking guidance from the Holy Spirit allows ministry couples to discern what needs to be said or done in any given situation. It allows them to prioritize their roles and responsibilities, while also being attuned to their own needs as individuals and as a couple.

If this applies to you and your spouse, take a moment and reflect on the importance of effective communication and reliance on the Holy Spirit in marriage and ministry. How can couples cultivate open and honest communication, and how can the guidance of the Holy Spirit shape their decisions and actions?

The journey of balancing marriage and ministry requires patience, understanding, constant self-reflection, and evaluation. It is not an exact science, and there is no one-size-fits-all solution. However, through open communication, the willingness to set boundaries, and a shared reliance on the Holy Spirit, couples can find a balance that works for them. The rewards of married couples walking alongside each other in ministry are immeasurable, as it deepens their bond and allows them to impact the lives of others. It allows their union to not just be a blessing internally but in external ways that impart life to others. Let us appreciate and support these couples who selflessly serve together, embracing the challenges and joys of marriage and ministry hand in hand.

Reflect on the concept of shared purpose within marriage and ministry. How does having a shared sense of calling contribute to a deeper connection and partnership between spouses?

Heavenly Father, Grant us the patience to understand the complexities of this journey, the understanding to support one another, and the wisdom to set healthy boundaries. May our communication be open and honest, allowing us to strengthen our bond as we face challenges together. We also lift up in prayer all the couples who selflessly serve together in ministry. May they find strength in their shared purpose and the joys that come from impacting the lives of others. In Jesus' name, we pray, Amen.

REFLECTIVE APPLICATION

1. 1. How have you witnessed the unique calling and contributions of individuals who balance marriage and ministry in your community or church?

2. Reflect on your relationships and the importance of boundaries. Are there areas where setting boundaries could enhance your connection and well-being?

_____
_____
_____
_____
_____
_____
_____
_____
_____
_____
_____
_____
_____
_____
_____
_____
_____
_____
_____
_____
_____
_____
_____
_____
_____
_____
_____
_____
_____
_____

DAY 18: BLENDED FAMILIES: FOSTERING GROWTH AND RESILIENCE

Dear Heavenly Father, we approach You today with gratitude for the gift of family. We ask for Your guidance and wisdom as we explore the unique challenges and opportunities that blended families face. May Your love and grace shine upon every member of these families, and may we learn how to nurture growth and resilience within them. In Jesus' name, Amen.

Psalm 127:3 (NIV) - "Children are a heritage from the Lord, offspring a reward from him."

Blended families, a term used to describe families that include children from previous relationships or marriages, are increasingly common in today's society. While merging two families may seem challenging, it is important to recognize that, with the right mindset and approach, blended families can thrive and create loving, supportive environments for all members involved.

One of the key factors in building a successful blended family is understanding that it requires an exponential amount of effort compared to a traditional family. This means that the same level of dedication, love, and attention it takes to nurture a family with the same mother and father must be amplified in a blended family. Stepfathers, stepmothers, birth mothers, and birth fathers all play crucial roles in bonding with their children, regardless of whether they are biologically related. It may take more time, effort, and patience, but it is possible to build strong, loving relationships within a blended family.

It is also important for parents in blended families to prioritize effective co-parenting. Once the marital relationship between the birth parents has ended, the focus must shift to ensuring that the children do not suffer as a result. This requires selflessness and a commitment to doing what is in the best interest of the children. Regardless of the relational dynamics between the parents, children deserve to have parents who work together to provide a stable and nurturing environment.

Blended families should not be seen as inherently more difficult or impossible to navigate. While there may be unique challenges and specific attacks from external sources, it is crucial to remember that quitting should never be an option. Building a successful blended family is possible, and there are numerous examples of families that have thrived, despite the initial difficulties. The key is to approach the challenges with anticipation, not dread, and to keep pouring in love and attention even when it may not be immediately reciprocated.

Blended families should not leave their relationships to chance. It is important to actively work on building and maintaining strong bonds with each member of the family. Children, in particular, respond to authentic love and care, regardless of where it comes from. While they may initially be resistant, consistent acts of love and support will eventually break down many barriers. Parents must keep pouring in love, even when it may feel challenging or overwhelming.

Navigating the complexities of blended families, divorce, and co-parenting requires patience, understanding, and a commitment to growth. By recognizing that love can be shared and that children deserve a chance to thrive, you can create an environment that fosters resilience and emotional well-being. Remember to give yourself and others grace, seek professional support if needed, and embrace the potential for positive outcomes. As you journey through challenging times, remain encouraged and keep moving forward, knowing that each day brings new opportunities for growth and happiness.

Heavenly Father, We lift our hearts to You. We are grateful for the wisdom and insights we've gained about navigating the complexities of blended families, divorce, and co-parenting. Help us to embrace the potential for positive outcomes, even in the face of adversity. Grant us the strength to create environments where love can be shared, and where our children have the opportunity to thrive, grow, and find emotional well-being. In Jesus' name we pray, Amen.

REFLECTIVE APPLICATION

Initiate an open and honest dialogue with your spouse or partner about your blended family dynamics. Discuss any challenges you may be facing and explore potential solutions together. Ensure that both of you are committed to working as a team for the well-being of all family members.

1. In your experience or observation, what unique challenges do blended families face?

2. How do you interpret the idea of "prioritizing effective co-parenting" within blended families, and how might this concept benefit the well-being of the children involved?

Reflect on a personal or observed example of a blended family that has overcome challenges and thrived.

DAY 19: YOUR MARRIAGE IS WORTH THE INVESTMENT

Dear Heavenly Father, we come before You today, thankful for the gift of marriage. Help us recognize that, just as we invest in our relationship with You, we must also invest in our marriage. Give us the wisdom and strength to prioritize our partnership and pour love into it daily. In Jesus' name, Amen.

"And over all these virtues put on love, which binds them all together in perfect unity."–Colossians 3:14 (NIV)

"Where your treasure is there the desires of your heart will also be."–Matthew 6:21 (NLT)

Marriage is a gift from God. A marriage that will stand the test of time requires our continuous investment. Our marriages require consistent attention and effort. They are living partnerships that demand intentional nurturing. Just as a garden flourishes when tended to with care, your marriage can thrive when you prioritize investing in it.

Amidst the busyness of life, it's essential to set aside quality time to connect and cherish each other. Your relationship is a treasure that deserves your time and attention. Understanding your spouse's needs and learning their language will enhance the bonds you share. It's also a way to learn how to love them effectively and cherish this gift God has blessed you with. Take the time to discover your spouse's language of love and speak it fluently.

As you seek to grow spiritually in your relationship with God, your marriage should also be a place of continuous growth and development. Embrace the journey, recognizing that challenges and growth opportunities strengthen your bond, and faith in God and each other. Investing in your marriage is a reflection of your love, not only for each other but also for God. Just as you nurture your faith, intentionally nurture your relationship with your spouse. Remember that love, patience, and commitment are the cornerstones of a thriving marriage. As you invest in your partnership, you create a vessel of God's love and grace, ready to impact your lives and those around you. May your marriage be a testimony to the boundless love and transformation available through Christ.

Dear Heavenly Father, we present our union before You today, thankful for the gift of marriage. Help us recognize that, as we invest in our relationship with you, we must also invest in our marriage. Give us the wisdom and strength to prioritize our partnership. Help us pour love into it daily. Help us find moments to spend together, to laugh, to communicate, and to create lasting memories. Bless our shared time and let it strengthen our bond. In Jesus' name we pray, Amen.

REFLECTIVE APPLICATION

Investing in your marriage is a spiritual journey of growth and transformation. As you nurture your relationship, you not only strengthen your bond with your spouse but also reflect God's love to the world. May your marriage be a testament to the profound blessings that come from investing in love.

1. How do you currently prioritize your marriage in your daily life? Are there areas where you can invest more time and effort?

2. Think about your spouse's love language. How can you better understand and speak their love language to strengthen your connection?

DAY 20: BEING A HUSBAND

Dear Lord, as we delve into the meaningful role of a husband today, we seek Your wisdom and guidance. Help us understand the profound significance of this commitment and inspire us to be present and dedicated in our marriages. In Jesus' name, we pray. Amen.

"Therefore a man shall leave his father and his mother and hold fast to his wife, and they shall become one flesh."–Genesis 2:24 (ESV)

Geoff

One of the early lessons I learned about transitioning from a single man to a married man came from basketball. Hear me out, when I first got married I liked to play basketball to stay in shape. I was living in a new city and eventually found a place to play pickup ball after work. Once I went a few times, a couple of the regular players would invite me to play with them more frequently. These invitations would sometimes keep me playing longer into the night than I had originally planned. I had readily agreed to play several times, enjoying the camaraderie, competition, and comedy that comes on the court. I hadn't considered that those late basketball evenings would end up disappointing my new bride. I hadn't considered that she was waiting for me to get home after work with dinner prepared, looking forward to sharing our night together. I hadn't considered the isolation my new bride sometimes felt as she was home alone those first few months. What I hadn't considered was how my individuality impacted hers. What I had to learn from those things I hadn't considered was just that… consideration. As a single man, I hadn't had to consider anyone else when making decisions. Now that I was joined to another, however, I had to consider my spouse in all things. Consideration for the other - a married man's responsibility.

The journey from being a single man to becoming a husband is a transformation guided by God's design. It involves leaving the familiarity of one's past and cleaving to a spouse. This cleaving isn't merely a physical act but a profound emotional and spiritual act of joining to form a covenant union. As husbands, we must recognize this shift and embrace the responsibilities that come with it.

In a world where relationships are constantly evolving, the role of a husband still holds great significance. It is grounded in a commitment to be present and dependable, to weather conflicts and challenges together.

When a man takes the leap into matrimony, he undergoes a significant transformation. Contrary to the opinions of some, putting on a wedding band doesn't instantly make one a husband. It is a gradual process of growth and adaptation. This adaptation is furthered by recognizing that marriage changes our priorities and how we navigate life. Our lives are no longer solely about individual goals but building a partnership with our spouse. The transition from single life to marriage requires effort, understanding, and a readiness to face challenges head-on.

To be a husband also means to be present in every sense of the word. This involves being there for one's spouse emotionally, physically, and mentally. In this sense, showing up fully in marriage means being present, even in uncomfortable situations or difficult conversations. It means being dependable and resisting the urge to run away when faced with disagreements or conflicts. These urges to flee are counteracted by a shift of focus towards being committed to the vows made before God and loved ones. By remaining present, a husband can foster trust, stability, and security within the marriage.

God's intention for marriage is unity. In unity, there is strength, and in strength, there is resilience. Remaining present in the face of challenges is a reflection of the unity God desires for married couples. It's a testament to the commitment made before Him.

Choosing to stay present and to work through challenges has a profound impact on the family dynamic. We can mitigate discouragement by apprehending the fact that conflict is inevitable in any relationship. However, how couples handle conflict shapes the environment in the union and ultimately for the children in the family. By being intentional about showing their children how to handle disagreements healthily, couples can create an atmosphere of understanding and resilience. Children are perceptive and soak up the positive aspects of their parents' relationship. Every effort towards reconciliation and forgiveness lays the groundwork for the child's future relationships.

Being a husband is a journey of growth, commitment, and strength. It's about recognizing the shift from a single life to a partnership, remaining present in good and challenging times, and creating a positive influence on one's family and future generations. The journey is aided by a commitment to dependability, thereby tapping into the power to remain faithful to one's vows. By embracing these qualities, husbands can cultivate loving and lasting marriages that serve as a foundation for a thriving family unit.

Dear Heavenly Father,

Lord, we ask for Your guidance and wisdom as we strive to be better husbands and fathers. Help us to be mindful of our actions and the impact(s) those actions have on those we love. Father, we ask that oneness and unity are built in our marriage as we develop consideration for the other. Please reveal to us the places of myopic narcissism that works against the unity you desire for us. Help us make the God honoring sacrifices which will produce a loving, considerate partnership where both spouses can find safety and peace. In Jesus' name, Amen.

REFLECTIVE APPLICATION

Think about how "consideration for the other" has been presented in your marriage. Evaluate areas of your life that are lived independent of your spouse. How can the decisions made in these areas impact your partner? Reflect upon the areas of improvement in communication related to these independent areas of your life that can help to mitigate the frustration that comes when consideration is not demonstrated.

1. What decisions have you previously made as a single man that now need to be made in collaboration with your spouse?

2. How have your responsibilities changed as a married man? Which of these new responsibilities, if any, have been difficult to take on?

3. What are some of the specific ways you can be present and "show up" for your spouse?

_____
_____
_____
_____
_____
_____
_____
_____
_____
_____
_____
_____
_____
_____
_____
_____
_____
_____
_____
_____
_____
_____
_____
_____

DAY 21: THE POWER OF HELP

Gracious Father, we humbly come before You as couples seeking to build strong and restorative marriages. We acknowledge the importance of seeking Your guidance and assistance. May Your Holy Spirit lead us on this journey. In Jesus' name we pray, Amen.

Ecclesiastes 4:9-10 (NIV) - "Two are better than one, because they have a good return for their labor: If either of them falls down, one can help the other up. But pity anyone who falls and has no one to help them up."

The conflicts that can arise in marriage can be exhaustive and intimidating at times. There may be times in your marriage you feel like you have hit a brick wall. It can leave you both feeling hopeless after trying everything to resolve an issue without success. It is important to note that you and your spouse do not have to carry the weight of your marriage alone: you have help. In John 14:26, the Holy Spirit is referred to as the Helper who can teach us all things. On the last day of our devotion, we explore the importance of seeking help and guidance in building and sustaining strong, restorative marriages. With the assistance of the Holy Spirit and the right counsel, you can navigate through difficult times and cultivate a relationship that thrives. A relationship that you both can enjoy for a long time.

When faced with the daunting task of overcoming hardships, it is crucial to recognize that we are not alone in our marriage journey. Building relationships that endure the trials of human frailty is challenging, but we are not without help. The key point to remember is that we have a supernatural helper and advocate (John 14:26 NLT). This realization paves the way for building restorative relationships, as we acknowledge that we do not have to face the challenges alone.

The foundation of a strong marriage lies in the belief that God is at the head. The Holy Spirit, as our helper, guides us into all truth, enabling us to forgive, let go, and overcome difficult obstacles. Without the ministry of the Holy Spirit, navigating through the complexities of marriage alone is arduous. Therefore, it is essential to embrace the possibility that building a successful marriage is not only feasible but also attainable with Divine help.

While the Holy Spirit plays a pivotal role, it is vital to acknowledge that sometimes professional counseling can also be beneficial. We fully endorse and believe in the power of counseling. Seeking professional guidance does not diminish one's strength or the power of the Holy Spirit, for that matter, but rather highlights the willingness to put in the heart work required to improve the relationship. It is crucial to understand that you do not have to face difficulties alone, regardless of the number of years you have been married. By embracing the concept of The (Marriage) Triangle (see Day Three), where God is at the top and the couple forms the other two points, couples can find solace in the fact that they are not alone in their journey.

There is a significant distinction between an average marriage that merely exists and a great marriage that brings joy and fulfillment. It is disheartening to know that some individuals feel trapped or stuck in their marriages. Many stay for their children, financial stability, or appearances. However, it doesn't have to be this way. By choosing to seek help, couples can break free from the mundane and create a marriage filled with love, passion, and true intimacy. It is possible to redefine the purpose of your marriage and embark on a mission together, where two united hearts can achieve far more than they ever imagined.

Reflect on Ecclesiastes 4:9-10: "Two are better than one because they have a good return for their labor... But pity anyone who falls and has no one to help them up." How does this verse highlight the importance of seeking help and support in marriage?

Heavenly Father, we thank You for being our Helper and Guide in our marriage journey, by way of the Holy Spirit. May we always seek Your wisdom and guidance. We also thank You for the gift of professional counseling, which can take us deeper into the heart and mind work we need, providing valuable assistance in our relationships. Help us to embrace the power of help and work together to build restorative marriages. In Jesus' name, we pray, Amen.

REFLECTIVE APPLICATION

Take time to discuss with your spouse the concept of seeking help and guidance in your marriage. Share your thoughts and feelings about how this assistance can strengthen your relationship. Identify specific areas where you both feel you could benefit from seeking help, whether through prayer, counseling, community, or other means.

1. What have the roadblocks been to seeking help in your marriage?

2. How has seeking help, through the Holy Spirit and/or professional counseling, impacted your marriage or relationships?

3. In what areas of your marriage do you feel you could benefit from more guidance or support?

_____
_____
_____
_____
_____
_____
_____
_____
_____
_____
_____
_____
_____
_____
_____
_____
_____
_____
_____
_____

Congratulations!

If you have made it this far, that means you have made it through this 21-day journey with us. We pray that the contents of this devotional will breathe a refreshing renewal, hope, and encouragement into your marriage. It is further our hope and prayer that you are able to take away some key insights to apply to your relationship. We recognize that every marriage is not cookie-cutter and although every marriage story is unique, there are common experiences that we all share. This devotional has been shared to highlight some of those common experiences. Although the marital statistics and odds are considered stacked against us we have been given the gift of God's sacred promise of His help and that He will journey with us if we let Him. It is our belief that with God's help, your marriage will continue to grow, thrive, and flourish for years to come until life is no more. Keep on loving and serving one another.

Geoff & Jasmine Gibbs

P.S. If this devotional has blessed you in any way, please share it with your family or friends looking to build Godly marriages and relationships.

SYNOPSIS

The concept of marriage is fraught with challenges which make it seem nearly impossible to believe it can be done in a healthy, long-lasting, fruitful way. Consider the challenge that requires two different people, who were raised in two different households, that may have had two different cultures as the basis for their understanding of marriage and family living together "happily ever after". These same two people process information, emotion, and identity in two vastly different ways. These differences impact the value they place on the other, on themselves, and on important things like intimacy, purpose, roles and responsibilities, love, honor, and respect. While the age old cliche' "opposites attract" may be true it does not guarantee it is a great way to start a marriage. In fact, it can make it feel impossible to build the things that are critical to having a lasting, loving marriage - unity and oneness.

This devotional is written to those who want a healthy marriage. It is a resource for those who are considering marriage and are looking for a guide to the stumbling blocks, potholes and roadblocks that every couple could potentially face along the journey to oneness. It is also written to those who are already married. The truths within are presented with a level of transparency that helps married couples know they are not alone in the challenges they face. It allows both husbands and wives to find language to describe both the highs and lows that can feel incredibly isolating, but which are in reality ubiquitous when two become one.

This devotional serves a valuable purpose. It gives readers a pathway to evaluate where they are in their marital journey, while presenting prompts by way of reflection questions that give us relatable options for our next steps towards personal and marital growth.

While it has been said that the journey of a thousand miles begins with one step, the authors believe the journey to oneness in marriage begins with each new day. This devotional presents one topic to be read each day for twenty one days. The truths for each daily topic are drawn from the pages of one of the most prolific sources of wisdom - the Holy Bible. One day at a time, readers will approach the question of how to build unity in marriage with respect to their unique circumstances by reading and hearing the stories of imperfect authors who are sojourning on the journey to oneness together. At the end of each day a topical narrative and a reflection question prompt the readers to consider how the truths of Scripture can be applied to their lives. As the devotion for that day closes, readers are invited to ask for Divine help through prayer.

The authors were passionate about writing this devotional book on love and marriage for a plethora of reasons. Their personal 26 year love story is filled with moments they share with readers, both good and bad, with an honesty meant to present themselves not as flawless but as approachable, relevant, and relatable. As local church planters and pastors, they have had the privilege of counseling and serving a wide variety of couples who faced seemingly impossible odds to build loving, lasting marriages. They have also been the beneficiaries of investments in their own marriage from God honoring couples who's unions have withstood the tests of time. Their unique insights are aided by their proximity to many couples who have faced nearly every challenge modern couples can face.

With a mix of humor, humility, and loving encouragement, this 21 day devotional will help readers build healthy habits which can turn the odds of building a life-giving marriage in their favor.

TWENTY ONE TO ONENESS - BEATING THE ODDS FOR A HEALTHY MARRIAGE

Twenty ONE to ONEness is a twenty-one day devotional written to married couples who are longing for help in building love and unity in their marriage. Written by authors Geoff and Jasmine Gibbs, this devotional guides readers through a journey intended to reveal the critical aspects of loving marriages. Each day, readers are presented with a topic that is common in marriage, a transparent discussion of the challenges common to couples on that topic, and a biblical truth that guides couples towards success in addressing these areas in their marriage. The topical discussion is coupled with daily Reflective Application questions which serve to help readers apply the truth to their lives in relevant ways.

AUTHOR BIOS

Geoffrey and Jasmine Gibbs met in Atlanta, Georgia in 1998 during their freshman year in college. Geoffrey, a Philadelphia native, is an alumnus of Morehouse College and Georgia Institute of Technology. Jasmine, a native of Hartford, CT is an alumnus of Clark Atlanta University. They have been married since 2003. For the last 26 years of their lives together they have faced their fair share of difficult obstacles and triumphant victories. They have been blessed to not only cultivate their own enduring love but have served to counsel and provide support for other couples on their journeys for healthy marriage. They have served in the ministry together since 1999 and have been ordained pastors in the local church in the Charlotte, NC area since 2015. During that time they have partnered with couples to provide premarital and post marital counseling. Together, they have 2 sons, Geoffrey III (Tre') and Jackson.

www.ingramcontent.com/pod-product-compliance
Lightning Source LLC
Chambersburg PA
CBHW071744040426
42446CB00012B/2468